SEA TURTLES AT RISK

by Megan McDonald

PEARSON

Scott Foresman

Editorial Offices: Glenview, Illinois • Parsippany, New Jersey • New York, New York
Sales Offices: Needham, Massachusetts • Duluth, Georgia • Glenview, Illinois
Coppell, Texas • Ontario, California • Mesa, Arizona

Every effort has been made to secure permission and provide appropriate credit for photographic material. The publisher deeply regrets any omission and pledges to correct errors called to its attention in subsequent editions.

Unless otherwise acknowledged, all photographs are the property of Scott Foresman, a division of Pearson Education.

Photo locators denoted as follows: Top (T), Center (C), Bottom (B), Left (L), Right (R), Background (Bkgd)

Opener: Getty Images; 1 Jan Butchofsky/Corbis; 4 (B) Peter Arnold, Inc., (C) Kevin Schafer/Corbis; 5 Animals Animals/Earth Scenes; 6 McDonald Wildlife Photographer/ Animals Animals/Earth Scenes; 7 Jeffrey L. Rotman/Corbis; 8 Index Stock Imagery; 9 Lynda Richardson/Corbis; 10 Jeffrey Greenberg/Photo Researchers, Inc.; 11 Marc Epstein/Visuals Unlimited; 12 C. Allan Morgan/Peter Arnold, Inc.; 14 David Young-Wolff/PhotoEdit

ISBN: 0-328-13255-1

7 8 9 10 V010 14 13 12 11 10 09 08

Sea turtles are amazing animals. They are large, air-breathing reptiles. Sea turtles **inhabit** seas around the world. They have been on Earth for millions of years.

There are eight **species** of sea turtles. The Olive ridley and Kemp's ridley sea turtles are the smallest. They weigh about eighty-five to ninety pounds. The leatherback sea turtles are the largest. They can be longer than six feet and can weigh 1,100 pounds!

Green sea turtle

Sea turtles spend most of their time in the water. They travel great distances using their flippers. Sea turtles have lungs. They must come to the surface to breathe.

Female sea turtles come to the land to lay their eggs. Did you know that a female sea turtle will travel hundreds of miles to nest on the same beach where she was born? Scientists are still studying how this happens. Right now, it is a mystery.

Sea turtle eggs have soft shells.

A female sea turtle digs a nest.

When it is time to lay eggs, the female sea turtle digs a nest on a beach. She scoops out sand with her flippers. Then she lays her eggs in this hole. She covers the eggs with sand to protect them. Finally, she crawls back to sea.

The tiny eggs develop in the warm sand. When they hatch, the baby sea turtles, called hatchlings, all pour out of the nest at once. They make a dash for the water. They come out at night to avoid **predators** that try to eat them. Once in the water, they must also watch out for sharks and fish.

Hatchlings must hurry so they are not eaten by birds or crabs.

Some people hunt hawksbill
sea turtles for their shells.

Sea turtles also face danger from
humans. Millions of sea turtles once swam
the seas. Today, all species of sea turtles
are **endangered.** This means that they
are in danger of dying out. One reason is
that some people want to eat turtle meat
and turtle eggs. Some people also like the
turtles' colorful shells, which can be made
into jewelry. However, many people want to
help the turtles. In most countries, it is now
against the law to take turtle eggs and shells.

As many as 150,000 sea turtles die in shrimp nets each year.

Another danger for sea turtles comes from fishing. Some fishermen use nets to catch shrimp. Sea turtles can get trapped underwater in these nets. When the turtles cannot get to the surface to breathe, they drown.

Longline fishing is also a problem. A longline is used to catch fish, but sometimes sea turtles take the bait on the hooks. The hooks can catch on their mouths. The turtles can also get tangled in the line and drown.

A crowded beach

Crowded and polluted beaches are another reason sea turtles are endangered. Scientists think that when sea turtles are on land, they use light reflected off the ocean to find their way back to the water. Bright lights from hotels and other buildings on beaches can confuse sea turtles. They might go in the wrong direction and become lost.

Garbage on beaches also confuses sea turtles. They might think plastic bags are jellyfish. If they eat a bag they could die.

Baby turtles may use light to find their way to the ocean.

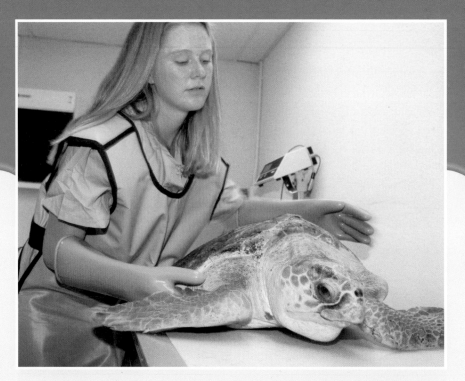

This turtle is sick.

Pollution may be harming sea turtles in other ways too. A new disease is killing many sea turtles. Scientists think the disease comes from polluted waters. Chemicals that run off into the ocean can pollute the water and cause seaweed to grow. Some turtles eat seaweed, and this food attracts many of them to the polluted waters. The pollution makes the turtles weak and they get sick. Some turtles get tumors and die.

Protecting beaches is one way to increase the turtle population.

Some people are trying to help sea turtles so they do not become extinct. Many countries have made laws to protect sea turtles. Some laws make it illegal to harm turtles or their eggs. Other laws say that fishermen must have special nets that let sea turtles escape if they get caught.

People are also protecting turtle nests. After a sea turtle lays her eggs, scientists move the eggs to a safe, fenced-off area. Then, they watch the nests so that nothing can happen to them. When the eggs hatch, they take the hatchlings back to the nesting beach and help them get to the sea.

Scientist in Rancho Nuevo releasing turtles to the wild

Rancho Nuevo in Mexico is a protected beach where many Kemp's ridley turtles nest. These turtles are the most endangered of all sea turtles. Since this area has been protected, more and more sea turtles have come here to nest.

All our actions can affect other living things. Some human actions have hurt sea turtles. We must **resolve** this **conflict** and work together to protect these creatures. Keeping beaches and ocean water clean is one way everyone can share the job. Careful fishing and protection of beaches are other important ways to save sea turtles.

Sea turtles have been around for many, many years. Let's work together to make sure their colorful shells will dot our ocean waters in the future.

Now Try This

Beach Buddies

You just read about sea turtles and learned that they are endangered. One of the reasons they are endangered is because of pollution on beaches and in the water. Imagine that you live near an ocean beach. Maybe you do! What can you do to make the beach safer for sea turtles?

One thing you can always do is make others aware of the problem.

Design a poster that could be put up at the beach. It could be a sign asking people to clean up their trash. It could be a sign that reminds people that sea turtles and other animals share the beach. It could be a sign showing people what happens if they don't clean up their trash. You decide! Use pictures and words to send a powerful message.

Glossary

conflict *n.* a disagreement or problem.

endangered *adj.* in danger of dying out.

inhabit *v.* to live in or on.

predators *n.* animals that hunt other animals.

resolve *v.* to settle, explain, or solve.

species *n.* group of animals that are very similar.